C000282585

STATIONS
OF
THE CROSS

Margaret Hebblethwaite

THE STATIONS

The first station
JESUS IS CONDEMNED
TO DEATH

The second station
JESUS RECEIVES
HIS CROSS

The third station
JESUS FALLS FOR
THE FIRST TIME

The fourth station
JESUS MEETS
HIS MOTHER

The fifth station
SIMON OF CYRENE HELPS
JESUS CARRY HIS CROSS

The sixth station
VERONICA WIPES
THE FACE OF JESUS

The seventh station
JESUS FALLS FOR
THE SECOND TIME

The eighth station
JESUS MEETS THE
WOMEN OF JERUSALEM

The ninth station
JESUS FALLS FOR THE
THIRD TIME

The tenth station
JESUS IS STRIPPED OF
HIS GARMENTS

The eleventh station
JESUS IS NAILED TO
THE CROSS

The twelfth station
JESUS DIES ON
THE CROSS

The thirteenth station
JESUS IS TAKEN DOWN
FROM THE CROSS

The fourteenth station
JESUS IS LAID IN
THE TOMB

The fifteenth station
JESUS RISES FROM THE DEAD

INTRODUCTION

A station is somewhere to stop and wait. When Christians make the stations of the Cross they stop and wait at points along Jesus' journey to his crucifixion.

Sometimes the stations of the Cross are set around the walls of a church. People literally walk around and stop in front of each, remembering Jesus at different moments of his passion.

It is believed that the stations of the Cross was a devotion that the Crusaders spread throughout Europe. The idea was to create an opportunity to follow the Way of the Cross for people who could not physically journey to Jerusalem.

Traditionally, since the sixteenth century, there have been fourteen Stations. They tell the story from the moment when the Roman governor Pilate condemned Jesus to death, up to his burial in the tomb that same evening.

To these fourteen sorrowful Stations is added a fifteenth Station, as a glorious finale: Jesus rises from the dead at Easter. This is the true ending, not just the ending of the story of Jesus' life on earth, but also the ending of the story of humanity's alienation from God.

JESUS IS CONDEMNED TO DEATH

 Pilate is in golden robes, Jesus in just a loincloth, with a purple cloak thrown over in mockery. Yet which one is really king? The artist gives us a clue by making Jesus stand a little higher than Pilate.

We all know we are going to die, yet that moment seems far distant most of the time, and it comes as a dizzy blow if a physician gives us only a few months to live. Jesus is here given only a few hours to live. Though he had known of this in advance, and forecast it repeatedly to his friends, we can imagine that the moment of signing the death warrant must still have had a stunning and disorientating power.

ECCE
HOMO
Gerard David
1450 – 1523

"*Jesus of Nazareth, King of the Jews,*"
   wrote Pilate.
That was the notice he ordered
   to be hung on the cross,
   to explain what sort of criminal Jesus was,
   to tell passers-by why he condemned this man to death.
Not much of a crime.
Not much of a reason for execution.
No wonder the chief priests complained that it should have read:
   "*This man said:*
   I am King of the Jews."

◄○►

Jesus of Nazareth,
   you are far more than King of the Jews for me.
You are King of the world,
   Ruler of the universe,
   Lord of all living creatures,
   Sovereign of all who have lived
   and all who are to come.
And more than that,
   you are the King of my heart.

I do not mind that you are barefoot and humiliated,
  while others are taking up postures of mockery.
I do not mind that when your purple cloak is pulled back
  you are wearing nothing but a loincloth,
  while others are in gold robes and fine colored garments.
I do not mind that you are wearing a crown of thorns,
  while others, in soft velvet caps, are deciding your fate.
I do not mind that your hands are tied with a rope,
  so that others can lead you out, and put you to death.
You are still the King of my heart.

Give me the grace to prefer humiliation to pretentiousness,
  the strength to choose poverty rather than greed,
  the courage to suffer pain rather than to hurt others,
  the tranquility to accept death when my time has come.
Let your royal blood,
  poured out for me on the cross,
  become my comfort
  and my refreshment.

JESUS RECEIVES
HIS CROSS

 Jesus stands out as a minority of one, and yet what power there is in this single individual, dressed in shimmering white, walking alone and with dignity toward the instrument of his execution. The crowds who had howled for his death fall back to right and left of him, lost in the shadows of confusion.

In previous ages, and maybe still today in some parts of the world, a prisoner would be left alone in his cell with the instruments of torture, so that the mental anguish of imagining what was about to happen to him would break his spirit. Yet Christians are taught not to shrink from the cross. On the contrary, they kiss it. Only Jesus could effect such a reversal.

CHRIST LEAVES
HIS TRIAL
Gustave Dore 1832 – 1883

"*Faithful cross*," "*noble tree*," we sing in hymns.
Hymns to the cross are very ancient.

Hippolytus of Rome wrote a hymn, saying that the tree of the
    cross is wide as the heavens:
      the mercy and healing that come from it reach everywhere.
It towers between heaven and earth:
      it becomes a ladder enabling us to meet God.
It is the foundation of the world, the center of the cosmos.
It touches the heavens with the top of its high branches,
      holds the earth firm within its roots,
      and stretches out its boughs like immeasurable arms
      to embrace all things.

Another passage by St. John Chrysostom says the tree of the cross
    is our nourishment and our banquet.
It gives us shade and shelter,
      where we can set up our tent in safety
      and find a resting-place fresh with dew.
When the tree of the cross flowers, we flower too.
We eat the fruits of the cross
      and its leaves provide us with clothing.

We honor the cross today in many ways. It is the most common
    Christian symbol.
Every church uses a cross as a sign of how Jesus Christ died to
    save us.
Many Christian books feature a cross on their cover as a mark
    of commitment.
Many people wear a small cross around their necks:
    it is a way of holding the cross close to us,
    of showing our love for Jesus
    and our gratitude for what he suffered out of love for us.
And so we can truly say:
    we love the cross,
    even though it brought such pain,
    because it is like a wedding ring between us and God,
    a token of a new covenant
    by which sins are forgiven
    and we are reconciled with God.

JESUS FALLS FOR
THE FIRST TIME

 The picture is split in half, diagonally. In the top half we see a sunset sky – even though we are in the middle of the day – because the old world is coming to an end. In the bottom half, Jesus is trapped in the darkness, under the almost immovable weight of the burden he must bear.

The gloom of impending destruction reminds us of what is about to happen: when Jesus is on the cross the sun's light will fail, and there will be darkness over the whole land for three hours. Creation itself grieves at the suffering and dying of the one through whom all things came into being.

CHRIST SINKING
UNDER THE WEIGHT
OF THE CROSS
Veronese 1528 – 1588

The end of life is painful,
  and the better the life has been
  the sadder is the moment of its close.
Sunsets are sad, and yet beautiful:
  sad because the day is over,
  the time of work and advancement is over.
But they are beautiful because as the light fades
  the sky is tinged with red.
As the light fades we remember the day,
  we think of what we have done,
  and of what we can no longer do
  because we are tired,
  and because time is short.
The gratitude of memory mingles
  with grief at the coming silence and darkness.

And so it is with Jesus and the sunset of his life.
Never has there been work of his intensity.
Never have we had such cause for gratitude
  as now that he is about to die.
Never has tiredness or weakness felt so painful
  as the tiredness and weakness of Jesus beneath his cross.
He can no longer carry it, but falls to the ground.

━◄o►━

Jesus, you have been a source of endless strength to your people.
You have healed the sick and raised the dying
    with the power of God flowing through your fingers.
Now your power has almost gone,
    and you fall to the ground,
    exhausted, drained, defeated.

Let me learn from you that there is a time for strength
    and a time for weakness;
    a time for work,
    and a time for exhaustion,
    a time for achievement,
    and a time for failure;
    a time for living,
    and a time for dying;
    a time for light,
    and an hour of darkness.

JESUS MEETS
HIS MOTHER

Still trapped beneath the burden of his cross, Jesus is now surrounded by his closest and most faithful followers. Behind him is the red robe of Mary Magdalene, whose love for Jesus has taught her to embrace the cross which is inseparable from him. And in front of him is the swooning figure of Mary his mother, who anticipates in the blackness of her dress the bereavement that is to fall upon her.

Faced with death, what is the least we can ask for? That we should be surrounded by our family and friends, grasping our hand to accompany us as far as is possible on the lonely journey of dying. And so Jesus looks with relief at his mother's face.

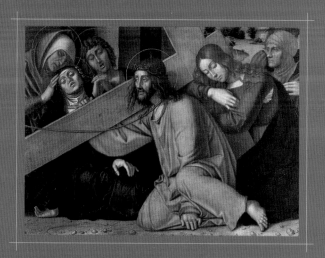

CHRIST FALLS
UNDER THE CROSS
Bonsignori 1455 – 1519

Can a woman forget the child of her womb,
   whom she has fed at her breast,
   and dandled on her knee,
   and patiently guided over the years?
No, for he comes from her flesh,
   and the love of the mother reflects
   the love of the Creator.

There was no one of the women who went out to Calvary
   who felt the pain as Jesus' mother Mary felt it.
No one who knew the sword pierce her heart
   as she knew it.
No one who showed such courage
   to see the worst as she saw it,
   the worst that could be.

What intimacy there is in love,
   to share the pain we feel as well as the joys,
   to hide nothing of our anguish,
   to refuse to shrink from failure, misery, and agony.
What love bound together Jesus and his mother
   as they met on the path to Calvary,
   and looked into each other's faces.

Long ago Mary had learned to say,
   "I am the Lord's servant,
   let it happen to me as you have said."
Long ago Jesus had taught others to say,
   "Thy will be done,
   on earth as it is in heaven."
Now those prayers have a new meaning
   as we take up our cross and follow him.

At the cross Jesus felt very close to his mother,
   and he spoke to her.
He gave her the friend he specially loved
   to be another son
   to comfort and provide for her.
He gave her as a mother to his beloved friend,
   as a mother to all his friends,
   as a mother to me.

SIMON OF CYRENE HELPS JESUS CARRY HIS CROSS

 SIMON CAME FROM CYRENE, in north Africa. If we look carefully at this picture, we can pick him out as a small, humble figure with a bushy white beard and brown legs, helping to bear the weight of the cross. He had every reason to resent the heavy manual labor imposed on him at the end of a long journey when he was tired. In doing a criminal's task he was made to look like a criminal himself, and he was chosen only because he was foreign.

Yet it was the best thing that ever happened to him, for he and his children, Alexander and Rufus, became members of the Christian community. Out of Africa came the man privileged to help Jesus achieve his mission.

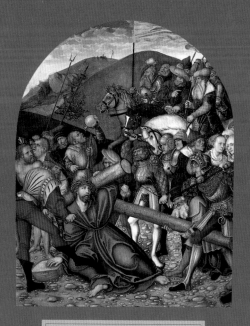

CHRIST
CARRYING THE CROSS
Lucas Cranach
1472 – 1553

What comes out of Africa?
Slaves came out of Africa,
though we are ashamed to remember it.
Simon of Cyrene became a slave for an afternoon,
given the work of a criminal on death row,
lugging a heavy instrument of torture up a hill,
as though he were a thief or a murderer himself.

What comes out of Africa?
Strength and solidarity.
Simon lent the strength of his body
to supplement the weakness of Jesus' body
after he had fallen to the ground.
He lent the solidarity of one marginalized person –
an African –
to another marginalized person –
a condemned prophet –
so that the two walked together as prisoners of their fate.

What comes out of Africa?
Rhythm and dancing and joy.
Move to the music, man.
Joy fills the heart of Simon when he finds out what he has done.

He dances with jubilation when he finds out he has helped Jesus
*   to carry the sins of the world*
*   and to bring healing to humanity*
He tells his children, Alexander and Rufus,
*   "Do you know what I once did?*
*   I helped Jesus Christ to carry his cross.*
*   I was with him on that day and I made it possible for him.*
*   Am I not the most privileged of men?*
*   Will you not join me and become his helper and follower?"*

◄○►

How often, O Lord, do we despise those we should admire,
*   and admire those we should despise.*
* Give us the freshness of vision*
*   to see among the developing nations*
*   those who are privileged in your sight.*
* Give us the wisdom to honor*
*   those whom the world oppresses,*
*   and the gratitude to thank*
*   the forgotten people*
*   whose labor has brought wealth to others.*

VERONICA WIPES
THE FACE OF JESUS

 A simple gesture, yet a vivid one, which has stuck in the Christian memory, though it is not recorded in the gospels. As Jesus struggles on his way – falling, bleeding, sweating, weeping – a woman comes forward to wipe his face with a handkerchief.

When people are truly in distress there is no help in telling them to cheer up. The only real comfort is to acknowledge the grief discreetly, as we do when we quietly pass a handkerchief. According to tradition, the compassionate gesture of Veronica was marked by a miracle, as the image of Jesus' face was left behind on the cloth.

A moment engraved in the memory.
A woman goes forward to Jesus on the climb to Calvary
  with a handkerchief.
His face is running with sweat,
  stained with blood,
  spattered with dust,
  and channeled with tears.
Not a pretty sight.
The clean white cloth soaks up the grief,
  and Jesus buries his anguished skin
  into its fragrant softness.
A moment of tenderness, of comfort,
  of womanly thoughtfulness.
A moment of gratitude.

Jesus leaves behind his thanks on the cloth,
  in the imprint of his face.
Before ever photography was discovered,
  he leaves behind his picture.
A special gift for someone who stepped out of line
  to show compassion for the despised,
  and who gave the little that she had,
  just a handkerchief for his tears.

Yet the moment engraved in the memory
  was not recorded in the history.
The woman honored by Jesus
  was not favored by the gospel writers.
The name of Veronica would have been forgotten
  but for a few who told her story
  to a few who told her story,
  to a few who told her story . . .
  until one day the moment printed on a handkerchief
  became a subject for a painting,
  and the deed that was ignored
  became a topic for meditation.
How good it is to remember that gentle moment.

◄○►

*L*ike Veronica,
  I will let Jesus bury his burning cheeks
  in the fragrance of my own soft, white handkerchief.
Give me, dear suffering Jesus,
  a memento of yourself.
Print your face upon my thoughts
  and your likeness within my heart.

JESUS FALLS FOR THE SECOND TIME

 Jesus has gone beyond his physical limits. He can no longer stand, no longer walk to Calvary, no longer carry his cross. He collapses in the attempt. And his head, his clothes, the ground, and the cross are all stained with his blood.

Jesus is the Son of God but he is also a human being, and he reminds us that failure is built into the human condition. He falls, and we fall, not once, but many times. The notice that will be nailed at the top of the cross reads INRI, which stands (in Latin) for "Jesus of Nazareth, King of the Jews." Even kings must fall and die.

CHRIST'S FALL ON THE
WALK TO CALVARY
Tiepolo 1727 – 1804

Jesus, you shared our human condition.
You suffered, as we do, the limitations of our bodies:
    hunger, thirst, heat, cold, tiredness, pain.
You stumbled as we stumble; you fell as we fall.

How humiliating it is to fall headlong in a public place,
    and how painful as we hit the ground.
At least there are usually people to rush up and say:
    "Are you all right? Is there anything we can do?"
Here it was the opposite.
The people who rushed up said:
    "Get up at once! Get a move on!"
Yet no one falls for the sake of having a rest.
Falling hurts too much for that.

Simon of Cyrene is no longer there to help.
The women – Mary his mother, Veronica, Mary Magdalene –
    would have helped carry the cross if they had been allowed,
But they were allowed only to follow and weep.
And Jesus' male friends have run away.

◄◦►

✠

Curled around the boulder that brought him down,
Jesus cries to God out of the depths of his despair:
"Father, hear my voice!
Why have you forsaken me?
Why are you so far from helping me,
from the words of my groaning?
Lying along the ground like this I am a worm,
no longer even a man.
I am scorned by others, despised by those around me.
All who see me mock me,
they make mouths at me,
they shake their heads.
I am poured out like water,
and all my bones are out of joint.
My heart is like wax,
it is melted within my breast.
My mouth is dried up like a potsherd.
My tongue sticks to my jaws.
I am lying in the dust of earth."

JESUS MEETS THE WOMEN OF JERUSALEM

 A great crowd of women comes out of Jerusalem to follow Jesus and to grieve over his fate. It sounds as though they made a lot of noise, for Jesus turns to them, saying, "Daughters of Jerusalem, do not weep for me, but weep for yourselves and for your children."

Women are so often ignored, yet they can be a driving force for change. In this painting they appear as a determined procession, indeed a demonstration, while the men stand around in little groups, looking on almost apathetically. This reminds us that it is good to demonstrate for justice, even when the action feels like a futile gesture against unstoppable powers.

What hat can women do,
   in a society where they are allowed no public role,
   where all the positions of power are occupied by men?
At the least they can make a lot of noise.

A great crowd of women came out from Jerusalem.
They wailed. They beat their breasts.
And in this picture, they sounded trumpets of protest
   and rippled harps of anguish.

How often, in television pictures from disaster spots,
   it is the women who are unafraid to wail,
   to scream, to howl,
   to show their anguished faces,
   puckered by grief and dampened by tears,
   and to let the world know what they are feeling.
How often, when justice is flouted
   and the innocent are murdered,
   it is the women who stand up to be counted.
We remember the Mothers of the Plaza de Mayo in Argentina;
the women who drove out President Marcos from the Philippines;
the women who started the peace movement in Northern Ireland;

the women who led the protest of two million
    against the murder of Miguel Angel Blanco in Spain.
"Howl, howl, howl, howl," said King Lear
    grieving over his dead daughter.
"Had I your tongues and eyes I'd use them so
    that heaven's vault should crack."

"Blessed are the barren," warns Jesus,
    "and the wombs that never bore,
    and the breasts that never nursed.
    For if they do this when the wood is green,
    what will they do when it is dry?"

◄○►

There is so much needless killing
    that all the wailing in the world is inadequate.
But we know, Lord, that you wail with us,
    so that heaven's vault is truly cracked
    and the curtain of the temple is torn
    from top to bottom.

JESUS FALLS FOR THE THIRD TIME

 Jesus falls almost headlong, his hand outstretched in supplication. It is as though he is begging, "Please … please." He seems to be asking for strength from his Father in heaven, more than for mercy from the soldiers. In his body language we can read humility and self-giving as well as brokenness. Above him on the hill the other crosses are already in position for the two bowed, disgraced figures who stand bound behind Jesus.

When we pray we choose a gesture like that of the fallen Jesus. We kneel. In such a position of humility and self-giving our prayer is to follow Jesus both to his death and to new life.

CHRIST AT CALVARY
Tiepolo 1696 – 1770

*W*hy is Jesus so weak
    that he cannot make it to the top of the hill?
Because of his vigil of mental agony in Gethsemane garden.
Because he has been kept up all night,
    mocked,
    hit about the head,
    crowned with thorns.
And most of all because earlier this morning
    he has been scourged.

A Roman scourging was savage in the extreme.
The "flagrum" had thongs of leather
    tipped with twin balls of lead.
After a man had been flogged repeatedly on the back
    with such a cruel instrument
    he would collapse and be close to death.
It seems that Pilate intended to scourge Jesus
    instead of crucifying him.
"I will have him flogged and release him," he said.
"Behold the man," he said, after the scourging,
    convinced that the sight of the broken, bloodied man
    would move their hearts to pity.
But the crowd cried, "Crucify him!"

No wonder Jesus fell, and fell, and fell,
 his legs weak,
 his knees cut;
 his back purple with bruises and red with blood;
 the heavy wood of the cross chafing
 against his tender, broken skin,
 giving him intolerable pain;
 his head buzzing with pain
 as the thorns pressed against his skull.
And all this before he was even crucified.

◄○►

See if there be any sorrow like his sorrow,
 as he falls on the stony ground;
 any sorrow like his mother's sorrow,
 as she watches her son suffer;
 any sorrow like the sorrow of the women of Jerusalem,
 as they wail for their Messiah;
 any sorrow like the world's sorrow,
 as we see the pain caused by sin:
 our sin.

JESUS IS STRIPPED
OF HIS GARMENTS

 In this painting of the disrobing of Christ we do not yet see the naked body, but our attention is focused on the loosened, blood-red garment that is about to fall from his shoulders.

Stripping before others can have multiple meanings. It can be the stripping before a doctor, that is a prelude to care and healing. It can be the stripping of sportsmen and women, after a mighty contest. It can be the stripping of lovers, to gaze on each other with love and adoration.

There is something of all those meanings here. Yet the over-shadowing meaning is of humiliation, as we prepare to see soft, warm flesh nailed to the hard, dead wood of the cross.

THE
DISROBING
OF CHRIST
El Greco
1541 – 1614

✢

Naked came Jesus from the womb of his mother,
  and naked he returns to God his Father.
Naked as he always was in the sight of God,
  he becomes naked also in the sight of the people,
  stripped of his clothes,
  of his dignity,
  of his reputation,
  of his hope.

Lord, you have searched him and known him,
You found him just and loving,
  generous and obedient,
  courageous and honest
  to the point of losing his life for the truth.
He spoke openly in synagogues and in the temple,
  he did not protect himself by speaking in secret.
All is made known, all revealed, all laid open like a book,
  so that we might see through his example
  how good is truth,
  how honest is humility,
  and how fearless is love.

◄◦►

His robe was seamless, whole and perfect,
    as his life was seamless,
    filled with integrity of purpose
    and consistency of love.
Even the hard men with their weapons
    could see the value of the robe.
They threw dice for it,
    gambling on who should be allowed
    to wear the seamless robe of Christ.

He laid aside his clothes
    as he laid aside his life,
    hiding nothing,
    holding nothing back.
He submitted himself
    to the gaze of those who mocked him.
He gave up his body
    to those who were unworthy to touch him.
He entrusted his flesh
    to those who seized him with iron nails in their hands.

The cup of painkilling myrrh he refused,
    but the cup that you gave him to drink
    he drained to the dregs.

JESUS IS NAILED TO THE CROSS

 Crucifixion is an obscenity. If it was not for the regularity with which we see pictures of the crucified Christ, we would find such images offensive to taste and decency.

But where is the greater obscenity? In the stripped, human figure flattened out and impaled on the cross? Or in the supposedly normal people around him who are overseeing the event as though it were all in a day's work? It is amazing what horrors people can take in their stride when their consciences become hardened. Happily we know from the gospels that there was at least one soldier there – the centurion himself – who recognized the goodness of Jesus as he met his death. "Certainly this man was innocent," he said, even "God's Son."

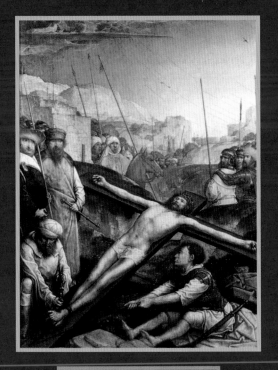

CHRIST RAISED
ON THE CROSS
Juan de Flandes
1465 – 1519

A malicious gang has surrounded Jesus.
A pack of hounds are baying for his blood.
They drag him to the ground.
Those who cried, "Crucify him!" are about to have their way.

The Roman soldiers do what they have to do.
With great professionalism they inflict agony.
They pierce his hands and his feet.
Nails are made for wood, not for flesh.

Can this naked, impaled figure be human?
Human beings are not found nailed to wood.
Surely it must be an effigy, as lifeless as a plaster crucifix?
It moves, it breathes, it twitches, it moans.
Surely it must be an animal, not a man?
At any rate it has left the world of humanity.
As one from whom we hide our faces,
    it is despised and rejected.
Its appearance fills us with revulsion.

◄○►

*O*h Jesus, you are still human,
  and this hurts you as much as it would hurt me.
You are still my Lord,
  and this crime offends God's goodness
  as nothing else has ever done before.
You are bearing the sickness of our sin,
  and carrying the disease of our bent nature.
You are wounded for our trespasses,
  and crushed for our wrongdoings.

◄O►

*"F*ather, forgive them," I hear you whisper,
  "for they don't know what they are doing."
They do not know.
They sit back now on their cloaks and eat a picnic,
  while you suffer in torment above their heads.
They do not know how much it hurts.
They do not know the good you have done.
They do not know the evil you have overcome.
They do not know who you are.
They do not know that what they are doing
  is done by the power of darkness.

JESUS DIES
ON THE CROSS

 On the cover of this book we witness the still and heavy silence of the crucifixion scene, as the faithful Mary Magdalene kisses the feet of Jesus in sorrowful love and angels catch his blood in chalices. Meanwhile, Jesus cannot move, he can only look on with gratitude.

On the page opposite we see the dead body of Jesus standing upright. It is a traditional theme rather than a realistic depiction. It gives us the chance for a long, contemplative look at the body, in a way that was not possible for the disciples in the haste of the moment. The sight fills us with pity.

THE DEAD CHRIST
Fra Angelico
1387 – 1455

You are still now.
A soldier prods you with the tip of his spear.
Nothing.
He digs it between your ribs, so your skin tears,
   and blood trickles out, and a clear liquid – water?
Nothing.
No life at all.

There is silence now.
If there was silence before
   it was not as deafening as this quiet death.
The scribes chat, the soldiers order,
   the thieves scream, the women howl,
   the dogs bark, the leaves rustle.
Yet all I hear is silence.

There is darkness now.
If there was darkness before
   it was not as blinding as this black hole.
The earth shakes, the rocks split,
   the tombs open, the corpses rattle,
   and the curtain of the temple tears from top to bottom.

The ground spews up its filth,
  and everywhere is dirt, bones, dust, stench,
  the rot of criminal bodies.

This is the hour of evil.
This is a land without God.

◄o►

But in the darkness and the silence
  is the memory of a breath of life.
A last breath, a dying breath.
A sigh of the spirit, a gift of grace.
"Into your hands I commend my spirit!"
A gasp that becomes a pant,
  a shout that becomes a whirlwind.
"Eli! Lama sabachthani!"
For as Jesus breathed his last
  he gave up his holy Spirit to travel the land
  until the wind and flame of the hurricane
  should come to rest on those who awaited it
  to burn them and to blast them
  into a new world.

JESUS IS TAKEN DOWN FROM THE CROSS

 What a touching combination of grace and awkward-ness there is in this dead Christ. Those who lament him seem to be gazing on with wonder and admira-tion in their eyes, rather than fear and turmoil. Mary gently caresses his head and his shoulders as they lie against her breast.

What a long way down it is from this cross. The agony has seemed unending, but now that all is over there is nothing left but self-offering. We see the relaxed weight of a body that has given its all and no longer offers any resistance. The example of sacrificial love draws the onlooker into the aura of its pres-ence, and the final note is one of peace.

LAMENTATION OF CHRIST
Bellini 1431 – 1516

This is my body, which will be given up for you.
Heavy with the burden of death
Heavy with the weight of sorrow
Heavy as the arms loll free of the nails
Heavy as the feet swing away from the cross
Heavy as the corpse is lowered
Heavy as his friends bear him to the earth
Heavy as he lies in his mother's arms.
This is my body, which will be given up for you,
    light as the touch of unleavened bread upon the tongue.

This is the cup of my blood, poured out for you.
The blood of the new and everlasting covenant
The blood of sacrifice, so that sins may be forgiven
The blood of royal lineage, of holy priesthood
The blood of one family, of sisters and brothers
The blood of pain, of sweat, and tears
The blood of healing, of health, and energy
The blood of scarlet passion, washing robes white as snow.
This is the cup of my blood, poured out for you,
    sweet and good as red wine poured out at the dinner table.

◄○►

His body lay in her arms, white, stiff, cold,
His blood seeped against her dress, red, sticky, lukewarm.
All the world was desolate now,
  for Life was murdered
  Meaning was empty
  Truth was mocked
  Love was destroyed.
And a sword pierced her heart.
She loved him with an overwhelming love,
  who was no longer with her.
She wept for him with unstinting tears,
  who had been snatched away from her.
What she held was an empty shell and a disfigured memory
  to anoint with oil
  to kiss with tears
  and put gently to bed
  until the new day would come.

JESUS IS LAID IN THE TOMB

 Here is almost a dance of death, as the disciples bind themselves to Jesus with bands of cloth and tense their own bodies to heave him to the grave. We are inseparably bound to Jesus if we wish to live and die with him, to be buried to sin and rise again to new life with him.

The tomb is a place of waiting. Without that three-day pause, Jesus' death would be trivialized. The body grew stiff and cold, and it seemed all hope was finally gone. Only when the depths are truly plumbed can we say that Jesus has suffered all that we have suffered, that he has descended into hell and broken its spell.

THE ENTOMBMENT
Michelangelo
1475 – 1564

I wait in the darkness of the prison,
   where there is no life,
   no light, no company,
   just interminable waiting.
It is damp and cold
   in this hole under the ground.
In time, if I wait long enough,
   the spring will come.
I cannot say when it will be,
   or how quickly the green shoots will push through the earth,
   or what shape will be the leaves,
   or what color the flowers.
I wake from a light sleep with a cry for help:
   O Lord, arise and show your power.
From the bed of the tomb I remember
   the word of the Father,
   in the dark and cold I lie awake,
   meditating on the promises of God.

◄○►

I wait in faith,
  where faith has been disappointed,
  and in hope,
  where hope has been hurt,
  and in love,
  where love is dead.
Waiting itself is all my faith, hope, and love:
  there is nothing else to do.
I lift up my eyes to the darkness above,
  to the invisible God
  in the unseen heavens outside my prison.
As a child looks up to his mother for help,
  so I look to my God in desperation.
I watch for the Lord,
  and I throw myself in trust upon his mercy.
My soul looks out for God
  more desperately than the night watchers
  who wait through a starless night
  watching for the dawn.
On a cold slab Love lies motionless.
I long for a living body's warmth and comfort,
  but find only a stark, sinister stillness.
I must wait longer yet.

JESUS RISES FROM THE DEAD

 But death is not the end. The end of this story is so wonderful that no words or pictures can do it justice. Because the resurrection is so hard to portray, artists use the stylized symbol of a flag of victory, with the figure of Christ floating into the air, his garments billowing in the wind.

"Look," says the angel, pointing into the empty tomb. Some people have no eyes to see, but slumber on in a tangle of bodies, oblivious to the deeds of God. But those who do see what has happened have eyes for nothing else. May we be in their number, our lives taken up with Christ in wonder, love, and praise.

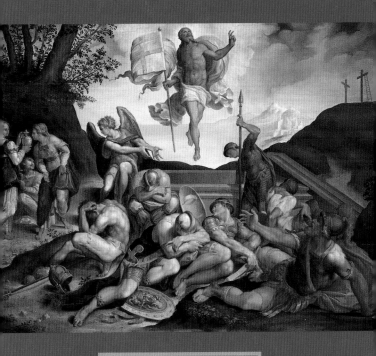

THE RESURRECTION
OF CHRIST
Florentine school
1560

✛

What praise can be enough for this moment?
What music loud enough for the triumph?
How can I thank God enough for this salvation?
How can I live with so much happiness?

◄○►

Let Christians make their offerings to the Easter victim –
    let their praises burn with fire.
A lamb was sacrificed to save the sheep:
    Christ, the innocent, has reconciled sinners to his Father.
What an amazing battle between death and life!
    The King of life was dead, but now he lives and rules.
Tell us, Mary of Magdala, what you saw when you went to the tomb.
"I saw the tomb of Christ, but he was alive.
I saw his glory, as he rose.
I saw angels, who bore witness to his rising.
I saw the linen wrappings, and his cloth from around his head.
Christ has risen. My hope has risen.
He is going ahead of you into Galilee."
We know that Christ has truly risen from the dead.
Victorious King, have mercy. Amen. Alleluia.

◄o►

As the light of dawn began to break
  our eyes began to see the world in the new colors of truth.
Blue for the clear, pure heavens,
  without a cloud on the horizon.
Red for the flames of joy
  that burn in our hearts.
Yellow for the shining sun
  that throws new light on all humanity.
Green for the freshness of the grass
  springing dew-decked out of the fertile earth.
Purple for the royal power
  of the King of the Jews, the King of Kings.
Orange for the sun-drenched stones
  that reflect the warmth of the Easter fire.
White for the radiance of his robes
  as he rises, spotless and unstained.
Gold for the brilliant rays of his glory
  now and for evermore.

✠

Copyright © 1998 Hunt & Thorpe

Text © 1998 Margaret Hebblethwaite

ISBN 1-85608-284-9

Designed by
THE BRIDGEWATER BOOK COMPANY LTD

Write to:
Hunt & Thorpe
Laurel House, Station Approach, New Alresford,
Hampshire, SO24 9JH, UK

Hunt & Thorpe is a name used under licence by
Paternoster Publishing, PO Box 300,
Kingstown Broadway, Carlisle, CA3 0QS, UK

A CIP catalogue record for this book
is available from the British Library.

Printed in Singapore

The publisher wishes to thank the following for use of pictures:
e.t. archive: p.5; p.33
All other pictures: Bridgeman Art Library